AN EMOTIONAL JOURNEY

A Book Of Poetry

CHRISTOPHER VICKERS
Jaelyn D. Jordan

Djs legacy incorporated

AN EMOTIONAL JOURNEY

Copyright © 2023 by Christopher Vickers & DJS Legacy Publication House

All rights reserved. No part of this book may be reproduced in any manner whatsoever without written permission except in the case of brief quotations embodied in critical articles and reviews.

First Printing, 2023

CONTENTS

Dedication   vii

2	Desire	2
3	Overwhelmed	3
4	Confused	4
5	Courageous	5
6	Disgusted	6
7	Desperation	7
8	Unhappy	8
9	Ashamed	9
10	Brave	10
11	Proud	11
12	Relief	12
13	Pleasure	13
14	Loved	14

15	Confidence	15
16	Grieving	16
17	Angry	17
18	Lonely	18
19	Respected	19
20	Disoriented	20
21	Valued	21
22	Tranquility	22
23	Hurt	23
24	Anxious	24
25	Grateful	25
26	A Little something new	26
27	H.A.T.E	27
28	By Grace Through Faith	28
29	I am who I am	29
30	Through The Looking Glass	30
About The Author		31

Thank you all, For your love, light and most of all support! By grace through faith!

DJS Legacy Publishing House QR Code

CHAPTER 1

Powerful

Times are tough,
The day is long,
The road is rough,
My mind is strong.

CHAPTER 2

Desire

The sound I see,
The feeling of a drum.
The blood from my chest,
The shape we all love.

CHAPTER 3

Overwhelmed

Tears of ice.
Tables and chairs, you can find me underneath,
Trying to be nice,
Grinding my teeth.

CHAPTER 4

Confused

The earth isn't winning,
I feel nothing,
The time keeps spinning,
My mind keeps buffing.

CHAPTER 5

Courageous

Fire in my heart,
Ice on my feet,
Holding in a fart,
A girl I would like to take out to eat.

CHAPTER 6

Disgusted

Bad taste in my mouth,
The blood from my ears,
The tongue from the south,
The mind behind the beers.

CHAPTER 7

Desperation

A stab in my side,
A desire in my hand,
A life I can ride,
Toes in the sand.

CHAPTER 8

Unhappy

Happiness can be hard,
Not much more to say,
Life will be unfair,
Spend time the right way.

CHAPTER 9

Ashamed

That look that I see,
The shame without a smile,
The way your eyes stare back at me,
The smile, something I haven't seen in a while.

CHAPTER 10

Brave

Flowers falling from the sky,
Tears I hold,
Watching the years go by,
As the time in my life will be bold.

CHAPTER 11

Proud

The look from my dad,
The ball I can barely see,
It's going far! Not bad!!
The sounds of cheers, for me.

CHAPTER 12

Relief

I stepped into the sun,
The light in my eyes,
The hope in the sky,
Happy the day is done.

CHAPTER 13

Pleasure

The sounds of birds singing,
The smell of fresh bread,
The feel of a little being,
Letting all the goodness get me.

CHAPTER 14

Loved

Everyone happy and sings,
Hugs and butterflies,
Wedding rings,
Bows and ties.

CHAPTER 15

Confidence

The time has come,
The clock is set,
The alarm has rung,
I gave it my best.

CHAPTER 16

Grieving

The time we shared wasn't long enough,
Never forget the sweet times we had,
When you left it was rough,
Forever, I will be glad.

CHAPTER 17

Angry

Why do you do this?
I'm so mad at you!
Broken, now fixed
I'm going out now, to buy some shoes.

CHAPTER 18

Lonely

I feel so empty,
Like a lost soul,
No friend to talk to me,
Like a cleaned-out bowl.

CHAPTER 19

Respected

Love you show,
Care is given,
The grace that we know,
With thoughtfulness we are driven.

CHAPTER 20

Disoriented

I can't figure it out,
What am I missing?
I feel like I need to shout,
I need a blessing.

CHAPTER 21

Valued

Favorite drink, with a lime,
Love in the air,
Curve balls of time,
No time to spare.

CHAPTER 22

Tranquility

The bottle in my hand,
My toes in the sea,
Together we stand,
As long as you are with me.

CHAPTER 23

Hurt

Scrapes I get,
Bruises in my soul,
Splinters that are set,
My body is taking a toll.

CHAPTER 24

Anxious

The time has started,
Now or never,
The sky has parted,
It's all coming together.

CHAPTER 25

Grateful

Pain and love,
Life isn't fair,
Watch me from above,
Always remember times we share.

CHAPTER 26

A Little something new

A little something new,
something I'm not quite used too,
freedom beneath my feet and laughter that makes my heart skips beats,
a little something that's not old to me but new,
a new memory I'm wanting to share with you.

CHAPTER 27

H.A.T.E

Hate an easy thing to do
Hate a word when mad becomes you
Hate a feeling that consumes your soul

Hate a word you have to let go!

CHAPTER 28

By Grace Through Faith

By grace through faith
Put him behind everything you do
By grace through faith
Honor him and he'll honor you
By grace through faith!

CHAPTER 29

I am who I am

I am who I am
No matter the flaw
I am who I am
Warts and all behind my face is true beauty
Behind these scars you'll come to see fully
See me for who I am
See me for my worth
See me for my heart
I am who I am
No matter the scars
Behind my face is true beauty.

CHAPTER 30

Through The Looking Glass

Through the looking glass you see a man
Able to hold and take care of his own
But within his mind he suffers alone
Told to keep working and pray the pain away
But the thing he come to know is pain and the more he pray the more his faith fades,
Scared and lost he took his own life
Because his parents just kept giving him tools instead of checking on his mind.

Christopher Vickers born May, 29 2013 in Tampa, FL. He is an aspiring child Model and Actor. As a young man he has only 1 sibling her name is Destiny. He is currently going through John Casablanca modeling and is being represented by Model and Talent Management. Christopher also has a passion for writing poems and stories. He hopes to become an actor, a model, an author and a role model to young kids and even adults. In his spare time he plays APA Little League Pool, Dad teaches him martial arts and works out with him, and he enjoys playing games on his Nintendo Switch usually Fortnite sometimes Rocket League. For those wondering … yes, he still keeps his grades up… usually straight A's and we couldn't be happier.
Thank you for your support!
You can follow Christopher on social media.
Instagram: @christopher.vickers2013
Facebook: Christopher Vickers
Tik tok: christopher.vickers2013

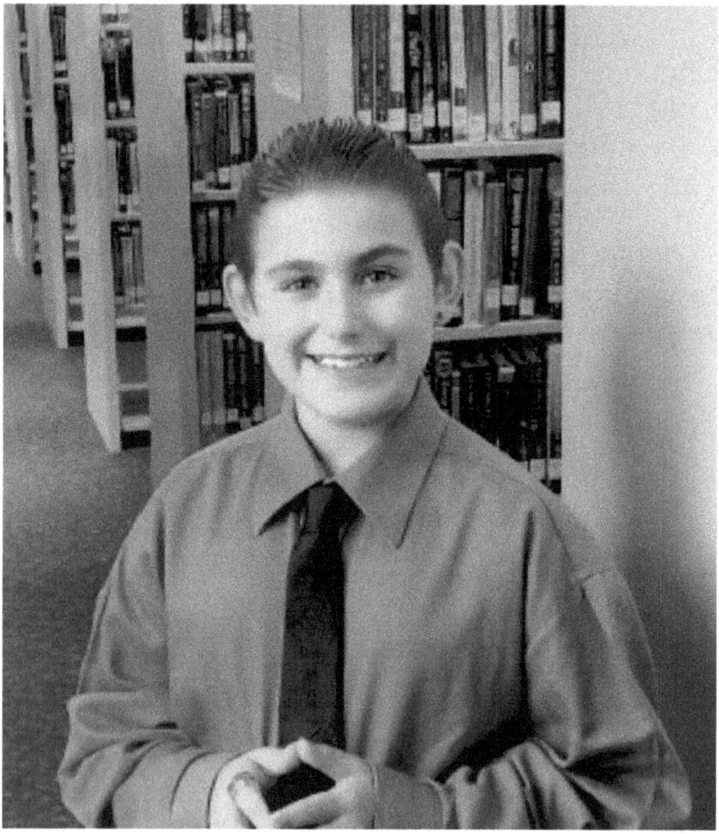

Printed in the USA
CPSIA information can be obtained
at www.ICGtesting.com
LVHW061315150823
754951LV00038B/94